For Roger
Enjoy

What You Don't See

With thanks
for all your support
Marty Gervais

Oct 13/2021

What You Don't See

poems inspired by making pictures

Marty Gervais

First Edition

Hidden Brook Press
www.HiddenBrookPress.com
HiddenBrookPress@gmail.com
EST. 1994

What You Don't See: poems inspired by making pictures
by Marty Gervais

Front Cover Image – Marty Gervais
Inside Images – Marty Gervais
Cover Design – Richard M. Grove
Layout and Design – Richard M. Grove

Typeset in Garamond
Printed and bound in Canada
Distributed in USA by Ingram,
in Canada by Hidden Brook Press

Library and Archives Canada Cataloguing in Publication

Title: What you don't see : poems inspired by making pictures / Marty Gervais.
Names: Gervais, C. H. (Charles Henry), 1946- author.
Identifiers: Canadiana 20210314877 |
ISBN 9781989786291 (softcover)
Classification: LCC PS8563.E7 W43 2021 |
DDC C811/.54—dc23

This book is dedicated to all my friends
To the old ones and the new ones
To those who are near, and those who are far away
To those on Earth and those in Heaven
To those who agree and those who disagree
To those I have never heard of
In the hope that we may all meet in the one Light

— borrowed from Thomas Merton

Table of Contents

I grew up in the newsroom, from my first days of landing a job at *The Globe and Mail* at the age of 18. I have fond memories of an old newspaper editor from the 1960s who would hold court in the newsroom, especially with naive cub reporters who were just learning the way around the structure of a new story, and this pipe-smoking curmudgeon would usually begin a long drawn out tale with, "Picture this ..."

And it's so true, for a story to have weight and be remembered and repeated, you need to see it. You need to be right there in that time slot, that particular moment to see it as the storyteller experienced it. This is the perspective of this book. It is all about seeing a story. It's about finding what's missing, what's in between. It's about opening one's eyes. The legendary Trappist monk Thomas Merton, who was given a camera by John Howard Griffin, famous for his book Black Like Me, said photography reminded him of all the things he had "overlooked" and the realization of this means that you suddenly experience "a strange awakening to find the sky inside you and beneath you and above you and all around you ..."

Marty Gervais

All the work is in the darkroom
Introduction by John B. Lee

What you don't see, what you cannot possibly imagine, unless you were there, and you were not there, is the day that the two photographers came to the farm intent upon taking photographs of my father's barns as they were beginning to fall into ruin. Dad had always been proud of his buildings. During the fifties, he'd had them painted red like most of the barns in Southwestern Ontario, a colour that originated with the blood-in-the-paint from the generation before when all barns in the region were red. There's an aerial photograph of the red barns with silver roofs, cattle in the fields, sheep in the meadows, bulls in the bull yard, board fences round the rams to keep the bucks from the ewes. And then he'd seen black barns at a Shorthorn picnic, and so he'd hired a painter to transform the fading red boards at home to flat black set off by green roofs with the foot high white lettering on the barn facing the road claiming the land known as Leeland Farms, for H.M. Lee and Sons. An image of those black barns fixed in a large, framed photograph taken from the vantage of a fly over hangs on the wall in my house. But those barns are gone. They've been cleared away, oak raftered hay mows, stone foundations, hip roof, and silo, all leveled and removed so the small hill where they once sat is raw earth, naked earth, with almost no story left to tell.

But the day the two photographers came, the barns were there, falling in on themselves, the livestock gone. And my good friends Marty Gervais and Bob Hill requested an opportunity to visit the farm in decline. My father, for his part could not understand what they were after. Why would you want to take a photograph of a couple of paintbrushes stuck in a bucket, or a stone kicking out of a wall, or a cobwebbed windowsill littered with sheep shears and twine, or a smock rotting on a spike hammered into a post, or a doorway swung crooked half-cocked on its hinges? These were the ghosts of glory they were after, evidence of what once was in the no-longer-that-way of chipped paint and a bent bucket, or horse harness grown mossy in milky light. *Come away from there, don't let them see that, and you must come to the village to see the mastodon tusks at the library, now that is a photograph.* These were my father's thoughts. *Don't let them see, oh please don't show them, and keep them away from there.* I saw a dead raccoon hanging by its ragged claw from the end of the eave, and I spotted another protruding where it bloated through the wow in a board. *I'll never forgive you son if you draw their attention to that.*

Soon enough we were off to the village where my photographer friends snapped a few obligatory shots of the world-famous Highgate Mastodon. For his part, Bob Hill was mortified but polite. He'd once told me of photography, "All the work is in the darkroom." And I'd seen the evidence of his artistry in his sepia tone prints. And Marty, who knew my dad well, gave him his due snapping shots of the seven-foot tusk arced and leaning floor to ceiling in the library wall like a weapon of war that might have been carried into battle by Goliath. And it isn't that what you don't see isn't there. What you don't see is manifested in the photography, in the stories, and in the poems of Marty Gervais. What you don't see comes into view, and you're grateful for the words that helped you see what isn't there, like those barns on the hill and the vantage when the poet Marty Gervais lets you look through the lens and says "picture this" and you do.

John B. Lee

"timing the feeling, and rush
of a new day, and this dance
maybe nothing more than
this, this easy refrain
maybe a life source
so easily mistaken
for beauty"

lines from "A Camera's Easy Refrain"

The Art of Telling a Story

My first day on the job at the *Chatham Daily News*
I was handed a Yashica-Mat twin-lens camera
a boxy metal contraption with a crank advance
and warned to keep it at *f16*
unless it was cloudy, then make it *f11*
and I had no idea what this meant —

and I went about looking at the world
head bowed peering down into a foggy viewfinder
that was at waist level, framing a blazing
fire, a rolled-over car near Thamesville
a children's play at a local high school
cheque presentation for the new hospital wing
a prize rooster at the Blenheim Fall Fair

and everything and nothing was important
and by nightfall I'd slide into the darkroom
spool out the negatives, dunk them
into solutions and pin them up with clothespins
to a line strung across the room
leave them for the photo editor

I was making art

I

Picture This

The Cure

I was not quite six years old
and I stepped out onto Ouellette Avenue
trailing my father, my tiny hands shading
my eyes from the dazzling sun
after my very first eye exam

I started wearing glasses two days later
and they rested unnaturally on my nose
like a sparrow dreaming of flying off
somewhere soon

and what followed were years
of schoolyard fights and cracked lenses
snapped temples, broken bridges, missing screws
and my father warning me he'd let me go blind
if I didn't care for them any better

But my brother cooked up a cure
in a comic book from the body builder
Charles Atlas, the man who claimed
to rip up a New York phone book in half
bend an iron rod into a horseshoe shape
with his bare hands, and now boasted
of curing blindness

and so my brother offered to lower me slowly
into the well at my grandfather's farm
near Stony Point and there I'd slip
into the cold deep expanse, wearing only a bathing suit
open my eyes wide under water for a minute
and a half — and that's all there was to it

I was terrified — I was 6
my head was swimming in doubts, if the rope
snapped or my brother lost his grip
I couldn't swim, I'd never get out

and so instead he calmly led me to the farmyard
to the well near the chicken coop
and pumped the handle till water gushed
and filled a rounded and wide tin pan
that rested on the ground, and told me
to take in a deep deep breath, dip my face
eyes open wide, into the water
and he'd count down the time
for the cure to happen
but he kept pushing my head down
my eyes staring into the scratched surface
of the basin, then finally lifted my face
from the frigid well water, and I scanned
the farmyard, saw the red blur of the hen house
and a zigzagging clothesline wavering
in the windy yard, and my dad's car
near the front steps of the farmhouse

and my brother clowning about nearby
laughing his head off —

I'd wear glasses for the rest of my life

A Sister's Death

I only found out my grandfather named
his mine *The Silver Belle* in Cobalt after
his little sister when I stumbled across
the Kodak Brownie picture taken of her
when she was laid out in a six-sided coffin
made for her by a man from the lumber mill
near the Ottawa River in Pembroke

She was propped up wearing the habit
of the Grey Sisters and my grandfather
told me how he had wanted to catch a train
back from the north to pay his respects
but the convent wrote saying it was too late
and instead sent this photograph
taken by the undertaker

and after a long time the picture found its way
into a small metal box kept under his bed
and that's where I found it, and that's
when I learned all this — I had so many
questions at the age of six
and my grandfather didn't mind
but from the Brownie spun more stories
about the dead — mostly unrelated

how he met an undertaker
from the Maritimes who learned the trade
by practicing on sailors with no families
around to complain, and kept one embalmed
standing up in the corner of his office
for a year wondering if someone
might come by to claim him

Now here I am seven decades later
and the picture surfaces once more
and I see my great aunt, still slightly
elevated like she's been reading
the same book all this time
with her eyes closed

Studies of a Five-Year-Old Watching his Father Drive a Car

I sat in the middle of the back seat
squeezed between my brothers who claimed
the windows — and my feet rested
on the driveshaft hump on the floor
but I had a better view of the road
and could watch my father
from this slightly side view of him
and as he drove I'd lean forward
and edge closer to peer
through the right lens of his spectacles
beguiled by the wavy distortions
in the curved road and gas station signs
and diners and passing cars
I studied how his hands shifted
the gears on the steering wheel column
up and down like a symphony conductor
all the while the dusting of ash
filtering in the soft sunlight from his cigarette
as it bobbed between his forefinger
and middle finger — I saw the way
he'd turn occasionally to say
something to my mother, a smile
breaking under his Clark Gable moustache
and how the lines of his face tightened
accentuating the straight-razor nick
on his neck — I let the sounds fade
so I didn't hear the gripes from the backseat
or my mother fretting over my father
driving too fast, or the thunder of wind
from the big open windows —
my eyes were doing all the work
the slightest gesture, the slope
of the suspenders over my father's girth
sleeves of the starched white shirt rolled up

and the tiny black needles on the face
of the wrist watch moving into
place in the slow motion gaze
of my imagination — my eyes
were doing all the work
in the gleaming light from the back seat

My Father Reading the Paper

Every morning he set the newspaper
down on the kitchen table
reached for a magnifying glass
and scanned the headlines
big bold *Franklin Gothic* letters
and from these he guessed
at the stories below —
now and again discovering a word
that he recognized
— that moment like unlocking
the grand puzzle
in the rectangular grid
of white-and-black-shaded squares

but he was never certain
of his intuition

Truth was in the eyes —
inherited macular degeneration
his father, his grandfather
uncles, cousins —
all of them living out
their last days
fighting blindness

Still some things never changed
his routine of reading the paper
— each morning he stared at the stories
a tangle of warped grids
of blurred lines
and words and pictures

After a while *Franklin Gothic*
couldn't save him
but still in those last months
he stubbornly and patiently
turned the pages

pretending

Family Movie Camera — ghosts of when

The film sputters and jerks as the image
fills the screen in this explosion of white
gushing at the open church doors —
white crinoline and starched white shirts
and bow ties and praying hands tucked
in at the chest, pointed upwards to the Almighty
and Sister Mary racing up and down
the aisles, poking everybody back in line
as Father Dill reviewed the First Communion Class
like Eisenhower, his bald head glistening
in the spring sunlight.

I noticed my sister moving into place
squinting at the sun behind me
and pictures snapped and my father's friend
operating a weighty 1950s movie camera
and finally, we pile into the Plymouth
heading for home, and there in the backyard
among rhubarb, late tulips we gather
for more pictures, a Sunday like any other
posing for the cameraman, a friend of my father's,

and I watch my father slide over to one side
to stand next to me taking my sister's hand
and I'm wondering whose hand I'll take
looking from left to right, then down again
at their clasped hands and suddenly I'm shoved
aside to let my grandfather in to stand next to my father
That look of bewilderment lasts only a moment
as my father's hand suddenly is in the picture
jutting from one outer edge of the frame
I see nothing else but his hand grab me by the collar
of my white shirt, and yank me back into place
I pull against his will, my face like a gargoyle's grimace
and wonder about those Sundays and all the people
in that picture — my grandfather with

silly Sunday pants yanked up high and belted
at his chest, dead now, my father sporting
a Clark Gable mustache, dead too
and a neighbourhood boy — not really a friend —
whose face popped just for an instant
from behind the corner of the red-brick house
and how he pulled back retreating to stay out of the picture
— he too, now dead, drowned one summer at Point Pelee.

Only my siblings are alive
my brothers and my sisters
We seldom see each other, seldom telephone
seldom write, seldom keep up. Now there I am
— a Sunday night in the basement reliving the life in
this old film, marveling at its grainy pockets
figures leaping off the screen like ghosts
of when things were never perfect
I am swallowed up by confusion
as if someone were about to reach out
and snap me back into line

The Boy with the Chess Board on a Summer Day

This morning as I swam in the cold lake
and looked up from below the dock
I saw a young boy playing
a game of chess with his brother —

the two of them barefoot
in bathing trunks, their focus solely
on this sport of silence, ignoring
the coming storm and its billowy
black clouds gathering like
an angry mob

yet the game went on — hands
in a pantomime of decision
moving bishops and pawns
in decisive worry over nothing more
than this balance of power

and still the approaching storm
edged its way across the cold morning sky
its shape reflected in the glassy
charade of calm

but I could tell the young boy
was entirely lost in this rivalry every
bit as real as the weather — and why worry
about what may come when what
you fear most is taking your eyes
off the battle right in front of you

At the Cottage this Morning at Eagle Lake at Sunrise

I left my grandchildren asleep
and tiptoed out of the cottage
on the hill just after the rain
had stopped, and eased my way
down to the dock — a morning
of blues and purples and dark shadows
and a tree line that glistened
with the sun rising, and the lake clean
and beautiful in the dark light

and I noticed how the dock stretched
like a familiar gesture into the cold water
— beads of a summer rain
still clinging to the cedar boards

yet still faint in my memory was the sound
of rain beating on the cottage roof
through the night and the monk
Thomas Merton speaking to me as though
the steady language of the storm
reminded him that the whole world
runs by rhythms we have not yet learned
to recognize and how the rain
will talk as long as it wishes

and now I feel its whisper within the silence

Blue Sky Snapshots

This recurring dream of a boy riding
a bicycle along a narrow ridge that juts
out into the sea, and I watch him
race along this windy precipice
my camera trained
on this reckless spectacle
and see him run right off the edge
arms and legs and hands holding
on to nothing but the blue sky
as the bicycle tumbles below him

and nothing

I missed the shot, so caught up
in the moment, I failed to press
the shutter — and nothing

I see the boy riding a bicycle
along a narrow strip of high grass
slowing as he nears the cliff edge
peering at the crashing waves
in a day so blue and somehow
when he looks up, I notice his eyes
like the sea below

and wonder why he lingers
and finally spot him
see him back up to start again
the bicycle obscured
by the tall grass, but he moves
with steady pace, shoulders and head
bowed intently, and the bicycle
soars off the edge, and I watch
how he grips the handlebars
to plummet into the sea

and again, I fumble
and nothing — too late with my camera
that sits like a stone in the palm of my hand

I dream again and watch the boy
study the windy path that brings him
back and feel the tires lift
from the shifting soil in that solitary
place above the sea where billowy clouds
have gathered nearby
like fans in the bleachers

and the boy sits straight up
as he sails over the edge floating
in slowest of motion above the sea
and I look closely —

in his hands, suddenly free
of the handlebars and purpose
is my camera, and now I am
the one in focus
in all that is blue

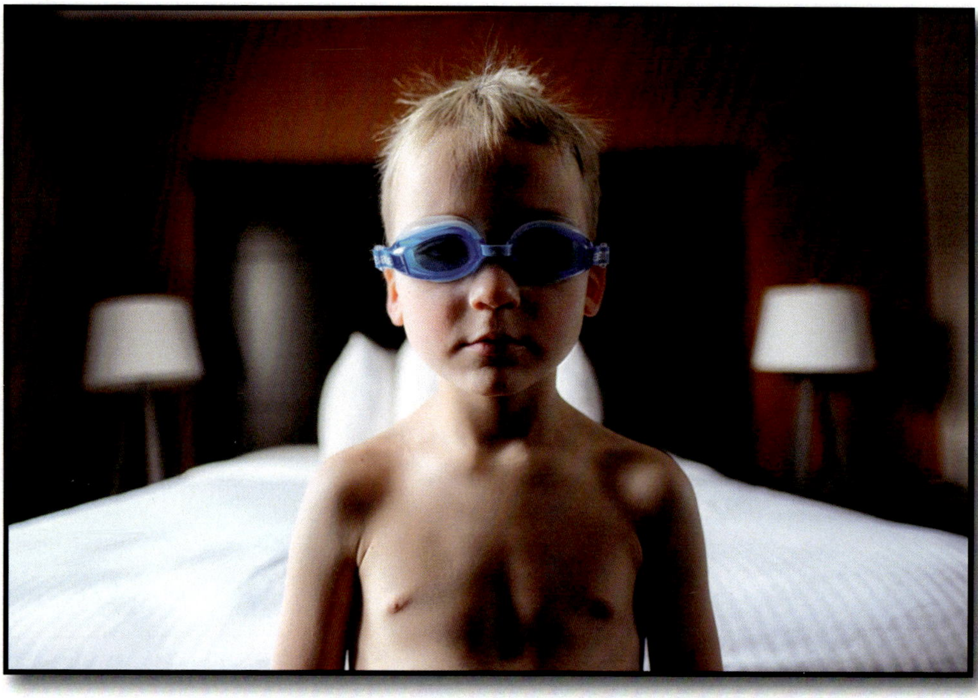

The Light is Never Right

The light is never right
and the letters are never large enough
in the book I am reading, and the lines
on the page bleed together
and my index finger no longer confidently
traces the bottom edge of a line

yet still I press on, and that's when
words the writer never intended begin
leaping willy nilly off the page
like crazed acrobats vying for my attention

The best and the worst of reading
is finding words that are not on the page
— a staggering subtext that betrays
a vastly different story, one never meant
or imagined, yet sometimes makes sense

Other times, I scratch my head
puzzling endlessly over why suddenly
the word "eat" appears in the place of "cat"
yet still I scramble and struggle and somehow
finally find a way to make sense of it

The Map of Every Day

His eyes had given out on him
yet he continued to move —
though cautiously through streets
to stores and coffee shops and church
counting steps, knowing
when to turn, feeling
his way to door handles
passageways, entrances

Still refused to carry a white cane

His eyes betrayed him at every move
— now having to navigate and rely
upon familiar shapes, deep shadows
cast by the sun, dark looming presences
of buildings — pictures to guide him

His was a life of expectations, routine
feet meeting tattered bedroom slippers
near the bed, hands guiding him
through ghostly doorways and hallways
brushing his teeth in a mirror
hearing tap water run in the sink
hands tracing the foggy soft shape
of a face, those deep shadows for eyes

and blindly staring, he spoke to them
cursed them, traitors, lazy bastards

My arms are working, so are the legs
so is the heart, lungs, and kidneys
you name it — all working
so what's your excuse?

his morning mantra
before he buttoned up his shirt —
fingers meticulously traced the edges
to line up the buttons properly
same colour socks, shirts, a fitted
plaid vest, a tie, jacket

and pens and a thick pad crammed
into a pocket – he scribbled notes
large childlike letters, sometimes
maybe three or four words to a page
fiercely intent to keep the lines straight

the words saved him every time
— they were pictures in a world
that made little sense without
this map, the silent voice

letters as large as Lego pieces

II

What Makes a Picture

Photographing A Wooden Bridge

For Bob Hill

I spotted him setting up a tripod that day
in the woods, and slide and click a Hasselblad
into place, then stroll over to a short
wooden bridge that spanned a narrow creek
where he reached into a coat pocket
to collect a light meter to calculate
aperture and shutter values — the device
resting snugly in the palm of his hand
while he paused for the sun to shift back
behind a cloud, and again took a reading

It seemed he had a way of approaching a picture
like a scientist, or maybe a tailor, or maybe
a surgeon, painstakingly and with studied intent
setting everything in place before finally
fixing the focus, pressing the cable release
but I was wrong —

he was more the poet, trusting the rhythm
the pace, the shift of stressed and
unstressed syllables — light and dark
each a language of its own, a simple bridge
as clouds drifted in, all that was needed
to sing and move in measured beat

What Makes a Picture

Remembering George Lee

Two photographers, a poet and an old farmer
went in search of the jawbone of
the giant mastodon that had been unearthed
in 1890 on farm near Highgate — it was on loan
to the village's public library, and the farmer
hoped his visitors would see it, get a picture
before it was taken back to
its home in a North Dakota museum

and the farmer knew the farm where
it had been dug up, only a mile away
and knew the family, even recalled
some of the fuss about the skeleton
of this great beast, but the photographers
had made the trip to meet the farmer and his wife
and they rode up the lane way to where
the tall black barn stood on a hill

That's what lured the photographers —
the barn, the hill, the rolling landscape
around Highgate, this family, the vast sweep
of the land and the solitary sun above

They cared nothing for the mastodon

Yet the farmer insisted on pictures
of the creature's jawbone dug up among
tree roots and rocks in a nearby ditch —
forget the photos of him walking among
a mob of sheep or standing with his wife
at the gate, forget the crooked fence
or the silent sleeping tractors resting
in the shade of the barn

and so, the photographers stepped out
into that summer day, and motored on down
into the village to snap pictures of the jawbone
of this great beast —

but went away puzzled over how
nobody mentioned the other creature unearthed
with the skeleton — the skull of a giant beaver
that had been the size of a black bear
with an eight-foot tail and teeth
the length of steak knives

Now, that would be a picture

Every Feeling Waits Upon Its Gesture

The photographs of Eudora Welty

I see this in the faces and arms
and hands of people
I see it in the places she photographed
in Mississippi — Depression era snapshots
of storekeepers and preachers
babies and bootleggers and sideshows
and fortune tellers and country churches
and jigging dolls and parades
and fishermen and hypnotists
her subjects these ambivalent
and forlorn boys and girls
and weary mothers on workdays
Saturdays and Sundays, ever polite
as she drove country roads to 82 counties
in the state, picture-taking by day
and checking into at end-of-day hotels
to scribble out their stories
— her words perfectly timed
to the drone of the noisy
electric ceiling fan

She said *every feeling waits upon its gesture*

And when she motored back to Jackson
to print her pictures in the kitchen
long into hot summer nights
it was only later in the morning light
she saw the ordinary but heroic faces emerge
and knew then she had somehow
imagined herself into their lives

and knew then she had never set out
to prove anything, to say anything
about the South or
the sorry state of the whole world

It fooled her, this camera —
but soon she learned to wait upon
that instant, that eloquent gesture
so stubborn and wayward

it was all there, alive, in the face
of that woman in the buttoned sweater
so full of defiance
more truthful, more terrible

Poetry of the Ordinary

With American photographer Keith Carter making pictures

He scrambled from the truck —
grabbed the trusty Hasselblad
with the Flex-body tilt lens
that gave his pictures that distinctive
sharp-to-soft-focus look

It was a juggler that caught his eye
— a man in striped pantaloons
doing a slow motion dance
on a giant carved head of a crow
and it took all of two minutes
with little coaxing, little direction
to get the picture

Then he wended his way to a colony
of costumed acrobats and jugglers and magicians
who thrived in the Santa Fe desert
a place of ramshackle buildings, an old yellow school bus
wire cages of doves, and someone
setting off firecrackers and flying kites
adorned with the American flag

Keith was entirely at home here —
photographing a woman with long blond
braids wearing a torn and tattered
wedding dress in the shade
of a twisted and gnarled Juniper

All of this he called the poetry of the ordinary
— the things we make of our life

Tale of Husbands

Based on a photograph by Martin Parr

It looks like it could be a literary salon
or groups of freemasons or Presbyterians
or maybe local aldermen
bitterly haggling over the merits
of sewer construction next spring —

all old white men and one man
sporting a tie and tweed jacket and standing
to patiently address the smoke-filled room

while the smouldering glow of afternoon light
burns and illuminates the slanted
and curved ceilings and the white hair
and bald heads of these serious
and assembled gentlemen

The photograph, in fact, shows
the Annual General Meeting
on Easter Monday 1977
at Hebden Bridge, Yorkshire, England

of the Ancient Order
of Henpecked Husbands

Photographing Lincoln

Mathew Brady's first portrait of Abraham Lincoln

Mathew Brady had always said
Take the picture now — you cannot tell
how soon it may be too late

and so it was that winter day in February 1860
at Broadway and 10th Street in New York
when this gangly smartly dressed, beardless politician
with a serious angular face and a high collar
fashioned to hide his unsightly long neck
stopped in for a portrait

It took all of 10 minutes
and that man was back running down the stairs
of the studio to deliver a speech
a few blocks away on anti-slavery

and this photograph on a single sheet
of glass soon found its way to the cover
of *Harper's Magazine*

a simple image of a man then unknown
now standing stock still and holding in his breath
arms at his side, long fingers reaching across
to maybe a Bible on a table

and who could know it would lead
to the telling of the grisly and terrible tale
of the war to follow

Seeing the Dead at Gettysburg

Alexander Gardner and Mathew Brady photographing the Civil War

The photographers rode in long after
they had already started burying the dead
landing upon the carnage with
their buckboard darkrooms and cumbersome
view cameras and tripods, and they stormed
into the smoke and stench, shooing away
hundreds of vexatious black vultures
that swarmed upon carrion mounds of dead horses

and maybe these picture-takers saw themselves
as no better, as they, too, scavenged
the stiff bodies of the dead
desperate for suitable subjects to tell the story
of this war, but still they fanned out to catch
the right light, the perfect angle of the sun

but the dead weren't always cooperative
— sometimes it meant moving the corpses
especially when they failed to die
in the right spot, often a better vantage
over there and *not here*, and so taking the pictures
meant lifting and dragging and hauling
the gory cadavers across an open battlefield
to reposition them so they lay posed
and properly draped in the foreground
for the cameramen — torn tunics bloodied
and slightly askew, and trusty
.58 caliber Springfields nearby

all the while gray smoke drifted and ascended
and fell back in among the dead accentuating
a sullen background where one might make out
a soldier stirring in the hazy distance
riding a horse in the aftermath of a battle

It didn't matter if this staging were all a lie —
as for the dead they found it hard
to put on a good face

Photographing Her Niece

Julia Margaret Cameron's photographs of her niece Julia Jackson 1868

They might've thought this woman
was a little mad when she landed all alone
on the Isle of Wight in 1863
and watched how she turned the coal house
into a dark room, then liberate
the henhouse she called
the Society of Hens and Chickens

and it was to this chicken coop studio
she coaxed painters, astronomers
scientists and poets, and one by one
they arrived to sit in the lovely
morning light as sun poured through
the glazed windows to soften
the edges of their lips and cheekbones

and so came the white-bearded Darwin
who leaned back and sported a black fedora
and Tennyson with stringy wet hair
a little ragged maybe from having
just stepped in out of the rain
and countless portraits of a bullied maid
posing as the Madonna or St. Agnes or
sometimes the poet Sappho
or there was also her husband playing
a furious and wrathful King Lear

but there were no props or costumes
or even posing for her favourite niece
the mother of Virginia Woolf —
the young woman was entirely herself
quietly sitting in the studio
that dreamy afternoon — wistful
beautiful, elusive, innocent
a faintly down-turned mouth
melancholic eyes and you can nearly hear
the photographer's words in that gaze
Beauty, you're under arrest. I have a camera

Pictures above Paris

The 19th Century aerial photography of Félix Nadar of France

The two of them squeezed into a
snug wicker basket, and he donned
a narrow-brimmed silk hat with a straight crown
and a flat top, and beside him, his wife
wore a simple plaid hooded shawl

and behind them a painted backdrop
of clouds in a swirling dark sky

all this, to announce he was ready to sail
over the city he had only ever seen on foot

all this, choreographed in a top floor
Parisian studio to advertise an adventure
in an air machine made up of almost 12 miles
of silk, and standing 200 feet tall — the size
of a small cottage and furnished
with a photographic darkroom
a café, a lavatory and a billiard table

all this, before he ever pulled its levers
and nudged a massive hot-air balloon gondola
up and high above the broad avenues
and soaring bell towers of Paris

never once considering
a simple malfunction would send
his air contraption crashing and bouncing
into a bog 25 miles from the city
nearly killing everyone on board

Yet after all this, he still believed
the folding tail-board camera
with canvas bellows would afford him
that buoyant moment to steer and steal
over the rooftops of the city of lights
and show the world here was a place
like a poem he had shaped
for its painters and poets

The Horizontal Line

Meeting National Geographic Photographer Sam Abell

He speaks about Ohio's clean horizontal line
of standing straight and tall and looking out
over miles of open farmland that fade into
a bluish blur while daylight softens its protest
let's down its cries to stay alive, and takes a bow
so twilight may gracefully move to centre stage

Those soft edges of daylight and nightfall
play before his eyes — this is what
brings him back time again, the horizontal line
balancing out all that trembles and defies
how he sees the world, even in the gesture
his father made as the older man rested
a forearm flat on a kitchen table, and leaned in
close to tell him something private

Or he might see it simply in the way light
traces a straight bright line underneath
a closed door in a room of shadows
and says this is as close to hearing an old tune
spinning its way back into words that spill
out of memory to shape the images
and tell the world all that is here
all that is alive and well and perfect

A Boy with Two Pieces of Bread

Meeting William Allard: American Photographer in Palms Springs, California

No need to scratch your head
to figure out his approach
to taking pictures —

look at the picture

A boy with two pieces
of sliced bread in his hands
blousy white shirt tucked
into sagging battered bluejeans
fastened up with suspenders

a buckboard wagon
in a field of yellow wheat
just beyond

It's the eyes you finally see
serious and fierce

an ordinary day

and you turn back
to those rough large hands
how delicate and careful
they are in handling
these two pieces of bread
lathered with honey

plain and simple
— that's how it's done

Window Shopping

A Depression-era photograph by Eudora Welty

...and it's suddenly obvious —
telling stories is nothing more than
a day of window shopping

and the window is the lens
we look through to find the truth...

I wasn't there but I know this
standing in front of a Mississippi store window
a morning with the shops just opening
and the help sweeping the dusty
street outside their doors
a hot and humid day just starting
and the sun filtering through the haze

and this tall lean black woman is poised
just there in front of the window
casual and confident in a cotton dress
draped almost to the ankles

and I wonder what she's doing there
left hand slightly cupped around her chin
in a studied manner, right arm crooked
back behind her, hand flat against her hip

and the narrow-brimmed straw hat
pulled tight and down as she idles there
maybe sizing up the way she looks —
that slim delicate figure on this hot morning
or maybe gazing at a pair of shoes
or a new dress or a skirt on the
store mannequin

I wasn't there and I don't know this woman
but this single photograph says so much
about storytelling and I clearly hear
Eudora Welty saying how the human body
is eloquent and stubborn and wayward
and the picture is a snapshot
a moment's glimpse

Building of the Ambassador Bridge

Sid Lloyd, a Border Cities Star photographer, climbed the Ambassador Bridge to photograph its construction in the summer before it opened in November 1929

He paused for a moment atop the world
to photograph the towering sweep
of the cold steel cables of the bridge —
Windsor in one direction, Detroit in the other
and the twin-steepled St. Anne's serene
and iridescent as a peacock on the American shore
Assumption Church hunched and sleepy
to the south, and he could hear the hiss
of acetylene torches, and see the men moving
easily in the open air
under a cloudy gray summer sky
and far beneath his feet the river
seemed strangely hushed except for
a lone tanker that cruised its way toward the open lake
and in that moment he didn't bother
with the camera — he kept it steady
by his side as he balanced at the edge
of one of the twin silicon steel towers
400 feet above the ground
— it was all too perfect
and nobody would believe it
and this would be the picture
he would never take

Final Portrait

Pat Sturn, renowned Canadian portrait photographer on her death bed

Her right hand gripped the railing
of the hospital bed like someone
clinging to the last fragment
of a capsized and splintered boat

and I watched her sink ever
deeper into those last moments
poised and acquiescent
for new adventure

She was one hundred, curled up in the bed
like a breath-mark in a musical script
accentuating how her twisted johnny gown
tightened around her skeletal frailty
eyes shut and face gaping up

She knew what she was doing —
petitioning no prayers, no mourning

offering only this frighteningly tiny frame
and upturned face and bony fingers
clutching the cold rail
of the high bed near the tall west window

and having the blinds drawn up
the afternoon sunlight happily lit
her wispy white hair and sullen cheeks

— this, a signature pose, the final gesture
of this one-hundred-year-old portrait photographer

III

What You Don't See in Pictures

Hemingway's Rifles

Photographs of Hemingway and his son Gregory
by Robert Capa in Idaho, 1940

Father and son at the water's edge —
a sleepy-eyed boy, barefoot
his left arm slung around a rifle
after a long morning of shooting pheasants
and father still in wading gear, leaning back
heavy boots, cap askew

Idaho, 1940, Silver Creek
and all this pastoral closeness
near the hunting lodge

the boy with two Winchester rifles
resting next to him, and his father, head bowed
maybe saying something to the boy

No past, no future, only now
and not a care in the world

while nearby the man's buddy from the war
Robert Capa — a 35 mm Leica
cupped in his hand — moves in to freeze
this moment, spin it into history

Throwing Away Karsh

A Karsh portrait of photographer Pat Sturn

Late afternoon in the summer
when I drove over to her house
to find her alone at the kitchen table
a large hanging lamp glowing
over her white hair
rough crippled-up hands
carefully sorting through old photographs

and she, shaking her head
at one in particular, a black and white
picture of a woman

— a quick portrait of her
from when her old friend had been
in Windsor to photograph Ford workers

a gift to her, this 4-by-5 proof
but she wanted nothing more of it
questioned what made her keep it
stuffed in an old shoe box
under her bed

now threatening to toss it away
along with a picture of an old boyfriend

The portrait was made by Yousuf Karsh
in a moment when the two met
at her downtown studio

and she now studied the picture
with a magnifying glass, barely visible
macular degeneration having eaten
away its edges, blurred her young face

Though that day in the studio
was still sharply focused,
she wanted nothing more of it
— *I never liked this picture*

Pictures on My Wall

1. The Manner of These People

The car door is open
and the sky beyond
stretches in a red glow
tired and ignored
for the light inside the car
bears life to the tattoo
on the man's naked arm
and you can barely see his face
as he pauses next to the gaping door
and leans down to kiss a young woman
who reaches up to say goodbye

while a man and a woman
in the interior glow of the car
near a half-open window
are kissing — it's easy to imagine
what they're thinking
yet maybe they're weary or sad
about leaving or maybe
they don't care to depart
but the man with the tattoo
is in no hurry
not like the sun that fades
quickly in the sky in its own
unremarkable manner

then again, maybe it's not
what it seems, maybe nobody
is saying why the man
with the tattoo
is leaving the woman
maybe something
has gone down
something terrible
or cruel or bad or wrong

Photograph by Christopher Michael Brown

2. Family in Their Car

The picture first appeared in *Life Magazine*
a husband, wife, son and daughter
sitting with a passenger door open
on the car and the man has his arm
around the woman who wears
a pair of jeans, and the daughter
in the back seat gently cups the side
of her brother's face, so maudlin
they all are, maybe sleepy
the way they seem, except for the boy
who is six or seven
— his eyes diverted slightly, alert
to something or someone
yet the wife is leaning back
resting her head on the husband's arm
this family so peaceful and loving

yet the real story is years later
in a place two hours north of Disneyland
on a pig farm, down a dirt track
through cacti, mesquite and Joshua trees
a place of no running water
no phone, no electricity, seven dogs
and the children in a nearby canyon
hide in a rusted-out camper van
amid broken glass, garbage
junk furniture and porn magazines

the picture on the wall
tells me none of this
or maybe I'm just not looking

Photograph by Mary Ellen Mark

3. Life in Gaza City

He grew up with the smell of tires
burning in the street outside his school
and when he was old enough
that sensation brought him back
to the streets to capture
the ever-present war

Barely 19 when he wandered
the neighbourhoods of Gaza City
after Israeli air strikes, carried a camera
to catch the moments that stripped away
all that speaks of truth —

photos of a Palestinian man with glasses
whose arms bear the dead weight
of a child's body drooping
like a wet-heavy carpet
or a woman in a stark UN schoolroom
and two of her toddlers asleep
on a twisted carpet on the floor
or a Palestinian woman with a bandaged leg
as she hurls a stone at Israeli soldiers
while gripping a set of crutches

but the picture that gives me hope
is on the wall — a father bathing
his five-old daughter and niece
amidst the rubble of what
had been their home

life as normal, as everyday
proof of the will to survive

Photograph by Wissam Nassar

4. Love in Pisa

This morning wending my way
through a labyrinth of tiled corridors
at *Cité* and finally reaching the *Métro* platform
I found the scenes of Paris —
sprawling posters of life in the city
verdant gardens and parks
and running children, and shopkeepers
and cafes and pictures of the coast
beaches and women with wide sun hats
dark rich colours, these massive subway panels
advertisements for an exhibition
this Flemish photographer whose father
told him taking pictures was sinful
It reminds me of the morning sun
an ocean away, and how it hesitates
in its path into my room and how
it brightens a small image of two barefoot lovers
awake on a single sleeping bag in Pisa
in the August light, and I remember
your words about how pictures
are not stories, but merely a question
of shapes of light and I can't help
but think otherwise for here's a man
without a shirt, a woman
in a sleeveless red blouse
both wearing rolled-up jeans,
maybe it's morning, they're homeless
and don't care about the camera capturing
this moment alone, or know how
they have come to live on my wall —
two nameless friends I visit each day
when I stop to see the sun
slip its way back into their life

Photograph by Harry Gruyaert

What You Don't See in Pictures

The photograph of Brig. Gen. Nguyen Ngoc Loan of South Vietnam's National Police shooting Viet Cong officer Nguyen Van Lem

His hands were bound behind his back
and he wore a plaid shirt, two buttons
undone and open wide at the neck
and a touch of wind played and flipped
back the bottom of his untucked shirt

or maybe it's the way his body twisted
abruptly as the man next to him —
a thin man with a receding hairline
in a bulky flak-vest — fired a bullet
from a snub-nosed .38 sidearm pistol
into his right temple

That is the picture you see —
the iconic Vietnam photograph
by Eddie Adams

a 1/500th of a second snapshot
freezing that look on the man's face
a fat lip, shocked grimace, eyes shut
and tousled hair

and a bullet crashing
through his brain at 600 mph

and the recoiled pistol
slightly upturned in the hand
of the soldier is like delivering
the crowning statement

all this in a single 35 mm frame

and some claim if you look closely
you can make out the bullet
in the hot haze of that first day
of February 1968 in Saigon

Yet it's the picture seconds later
you never see — the thin man with the pistol
slipping it back into his holster as casual
as tucking away a wallet after buying a coffee

or the man in the plaid shirt, slumped
in a pool of blood on the pavement
like a curled-up safari kill
skinny legs and bare feet

It's the picture you never see
the man with the pistol years later
sleeves rolled up to the elbows
just like that day in February heat of Saigon
now smiling and leaning
at a lunch counter in the pizzeria
he opened near Washington D.C.

But pictures tell only *half-truths*
says Eddie Adams — they never
tell the whole story

Two Pictures of the Last Man To Die

Robert Capa's photograph from Life Magazine *May 14, 1945*

He was photographed just before
he was shot in the forehead
by a German sniper

It is this first picture of this soldier
that made me wonder —
what crossed his mind as he idled
in the morning sunshine of an open balcony
on the second floor of this yellow-stone building
just above an intersection in Leipzig

one minute dream-eyeing the scene below
and feeding a heavy M1 Garand machine gun

the next moment in a second photograph
fallen back onto the parquet floor
— a pool of blood spreading out
like a dark shadow in the harsh daytime light

It was one of the last days of the war

And seeing this photograph from *Life Magazine*
I can almost hear the photographer
frantically scrambling up a nearby balcony
to climb through and into the room
finally emerging to spot the soldier
lying back, still wearing the looted
Luftwaffe sheepskin helmet

I hear him tell the platoon leader
It was a clean, somehow very beautiful death

Vladimir Horowitz: The American Tour Resumes in Detroit After the Death of His Mother

He was six when his mother slid in beside him
at the piano in the parlour in Kiev to guide
his hands over the vast array of gleaming black
and white keys, and now the warm glow
of a single stage light enveloped
the imposing nine-foot Steinway that broods
like a *Toro Bravo* in the Iberian sunlight

and there he was — a tall yet short-waisted man
walking slowly to the edge of the stage to pause
and bow and tell his audience this performance
would be for his mother, his first piano teacher

I didn't notice right away when he turned briskly
to move to the piano bench and sit all the way
to one side — ungainly and not perfectly lined up
but then again, his hands always tilted down
palms slightly below the level of the Steinway's
gleaming Bavarian spruce keys, nearly cupping
the edge, playing chords with straight fingers
and always the little finger of his right hand
it was said, curiously curled up and ready
to strike like a cobra — I didn't notice
until he had started in, and then spotted
that awkward gap, the place beside him, empty
but now for the ghost of his mother taking
her young boy through the moment
guiding him in all the radiance of his return

Boys of Summer

Based on a photograph by Sid Lloyd

Summer of 1934 and he didn't live far —
just a few blocks running up from the river
and he knew he could reach the ferry boat
as it departed Walkerville
and catch the swimmers climbing
the three-decker as it set out
to take its riders to Detroit

and he stood on the river's south bank
waited for them, steadied his 4X5 Speed Graphic
and snapped one exposure before
sliding in another film holder and switching out
the dark slide, cocking the focal plane shutter
and clicked, and there was the moment
— four fellows on a July afternoon diving
from the ferry, arms stretched in flight
to feel the wind, bodies rigid and disciplined
in this caper, and he wondered
how intuitive were their limbs as they gracefully
opened wide like the petals of spring magnolias
then tightened and narrowed before
plunging headlong into the warm river

Today I see this vintage picture, and realize
this man nearby with a camera somehow
has fixed and frozen these boys in all
that momentary wonder as they leapt
off the rails of the ferry, their carefree youth
believing nothing could ever capture
how a summer day might bring such joy

IV

How a Picture is Made

First Sight October 1946

The moment of my birth
a stream of sunlight on the ceiling
late October, daytime, first light
abstract wonder in all its magic
and shadows coming and going
a Sunday morning, with first sounds
like soft haloes and brightness so pure

The Man Without Blood

Photograph by Father William Kornacker in Peru 1981

I can still feel the little boy's arms
wrapped tightly around my midriff
as the two of us rode a rickety bicycle
along a dirt road into this town
in the Zana Valley

and the children were running
beside me, and laughing
and mothers stepped out of doorways
to greet my arrival, and a parish priest
moved in to snap a photo

and all these years later
the magic is in clearly
picturing the ensuing moments
the next frames of that camera
clicking away to capture
the village children and catch
them huddle in the open street
as I flew past, and spied them
point and heard them snicker
at how white was my skin
this ghost on wheels

and felt the shutter freeze
the unmistakable steady cadence
of their chant
el hombre sin sangre!
el hombre sin sangre!

How to Make a Picture

Based on a story by Cathy Lee

We were both hit by a car as children
I was maybe five, and you were eight
and for me it is a blur, one moment
racing with a mouth bulging with bubble gum
into a sunny street between two parked cars
the next, rousing awake to the wail of sirens
in an ambulance before tumbling back to sleep
before blinking awake again to a glare
of lights in my eyes and later cruising home
stretched out on the back seat of my father's car
along a lilac-lined driveway in that place
not far from the river

and my eyes photographing fogged
and distorted images of trees and a blue
sky through the landscape-shaped window
of my father's new Ford

But yours was a day like any other
and as you reach back to the details
of lying in the hospital — I see my hands
yearn to separate and comb out long strands
of blond hair snarled and twisted
over your eyes, a fierce tangle of mud
and blood, and I watch doctors hover
with slit-lamps and I catch your blue eyes
flutter open through the mess
and in that instant I have this picture
so full of mystery and confusion
you this little girl, hurt and broken
and captured and spinning forever
in a sea of white and all its purity

Light in the Morning

I stand in the morning light
peering up at the leafless Black Oaks
stretching heavenward
and for a moment I believe
they applaud my arrival
or it's maybe the wind

but it's the light
over the land and the woods
that I hear moving in to tell me
to pay attention

It's the light in the trees
Thomas Merton described
as *pure and simple*

It's the light that breaks
the bleak weather and gives
strength to the trees
as they wake to the spring

Photographing a Trappist Monk

For Br. Paul Quenon

It is easy to capture him, to see him leap
across bales of hay, this Trappist monk
in a rolling field shorn of its wealth
as he moves like a left fielder to catch
this long drive, legs stretching as if
he is running out of time
It is easy to see him — he is going
nowhere but into a blue sky
and what does God say and the sky speak

A Camera's Easy Refrain

I spent the entire morning sitting
on the tiled floor of the bathroom
photographing the curtain
as it billowed out with the spring
breeze, this ghostly textured
apparition that was telling me
something of its grace
its elegance in the coolness
of a morning, sun-rich
and joyful, this breathing shape
rising full and healthy in its reach
and slowly settling back
and the only sound, a camera
shutter like a metronome
timing the feeling and rush
of a new day, and this dance
maybe nothing more than
this, this easy refrain
maybe a life source
so easily mistaken
for beauty

Picture in the Paper

That morning just before Christmas
in 1958 my friend piled into the car
with his mother, his brother
and two sisters and the baby
all into the big Chrysler, the one
my father said had that egg-crate grill
and his mother headed out into the ice storm
maybe in a bit of a hurry
and as she sped over the iron bridge
near the railway station
the car skidded and crashed
through the railings and plunged
into the river — I remember that day
at school because my friend
who sat adjacent to me in Grade 7
was absent that morning

and by recess we heard his mother
and siblings had all perished
in the icy Muskoka River

I saved the picture of the bridge
from the next day's newspaper
eased and folded it into my coat pocket
and carried it with me, and later
went down to the bridge
took out the picture

and stared at it above the rapids
could not help but see the faces
of the children and my friend
in the wide sweep of windows
as the car sank into the cold river

I saw it clearly in the photograph
every time I unfolded it

Shooting Dogs

I never could shoot the coyotes
though I joined my neighbours
who tracked and hunted them down
through wind-swept winter fields of Essex County
I rode with those farmers in the cab of
bumpy smoky pickups, windows wide open
rifles held beside, the trucks racing
along concession roads as we drove
herding those coy-dogs across stubbled fields

I watched these hunters pile out
of their trucks to stand alongside the road
lined up like soldiers — cold rifles
trained on the coyotes, and one by one
these doomed creatures rushed into
their gun-sights, tumbling and squealing

but one coyote sped between the lineup
raced past the trucks into the open flats and beyond
as the farmers followed, each raising his rifle
but the wind was strong and they let that brush wolf go —
and I watched it disappear into
the far off snowy field's horizon running
for all its life, never once looking back

When I turned around, I saw the men
lighting up cigars, rifles balanced on forearms
celebrating their victory before moving
into the late windy afternoon to collect the kill
and toss each carcass into the bed of their pickups

Later I stopped by a neighbour's barn
surprised to see these stiff-bodied coyotes
dangling from hooks
and photographed them for the paper
and heard startling tales of how these coyotes
raided chicken coops, dragged off family pets
you name the harm they'd done …

and I snapped a dozen pictures, moving in and out
and around and through the cold barn, half listening
to the chatter among the men drinking beer
and thought *I'm really no better than them*
— *I'm shooting coyotes too*

Finally I hopped into my car, felt it shudder, then start
and headed home to a spit-gray cold January sky
daydreaming and feeling low, and was maybe
a half mile from my place, and started fiddling
with the radio to tune in the news
when out of the corner of my eye
there was a coyote crouching
at the edge of the ditch

I stopped, lowered my window
— the lone coyote didn't budge — I studied
his narrow, elongated snout, his lean body
his bushy tail, thick fur, and his yellow eyes
— I did not dare to take his picture

The Ice Box

When you tell me this
and show me pictures of your father
at the river's edge in the clapboard cottage
I imagine a slate-grey misty morning

and you, a young girl, at the porch window
watching your father lift up
an old white zinc icebox upon his wide shoulders
and step barefoot to the river's edge

and study him slowly descend chest deep
then stop and nudge the icebox
a little higher, arms finally lifting it
up and off his bare shoulders
and above his head

like Atlas bearing the full weight
of the celestial heavens and all its stories

and I see it topple into the deepest part
of the river, catch it slip into the channel
where the river meets the lake

I want to follow it, picture it roll
and tumble in slow motion and find
its way to the bottom, into a river graveyard
of beer bottles, whiskey crates, old jalopies

and now this summer ice box lies open
and awake to spill out its own tales

The Shepherd's Square Dance

For George Lee

The picture I took is all that survives
of that moment when there was still
sheep and cattle and hogs and chickens
and acres of lush pastureland that stretched
out to the fences that defined a family

and it was the straw hat that I saw
and the way the man moved, his head
tilted down as he approached the sheep
left hand gripping the handle
of a feed bucket, hips swaying and legs
and feet in tattered loosely laced work boots
moving in a do-si-do dance step
while the sheep circled round
to a half sashay then back-to-back
all the while the man in the straw hat
called the steps

I swear you could almost hear the music
as the black barns thrummed
in the afternoon sun

Thomas Merton's Cameras

Staying for a week at the Hermitage at the Abbey of Gethsemani, Trappist, Kentucky

There I was, a windy winter night in January
cold rain pummeling me as I rushed up
this muddy incline to the Kentucky cabin
past a large wooden cross overlooking
the eaves of the hermitage —

I brought along a notebook and pens
a couple of books in a satchel
but also a camera, and it occurred to me
within an hour the difficult challenge
of turning my first impressions
into 35 mm film

So where do I start?

How do I photograph the stillness?
How do I capture the coyotes howling
all night outside my cabin? How do
I replicate the sound of rain, January
thunder? The crackling wood in the
fireplace and the desperation to keep warm?

Thomas Merton lived here
and borrowed a 35 mm Canon FX
from John Howard Griffin
and turned a studied eye
toward details all around him
ordinary objects, everyday tools
he might've taken for granted
a hammer, a shovel, bark
from a sassafras tree, leaves
and rocks, wagon wheels, the pail
just outside the screen door
and two large muddy Wellingtons
tipped over on the porch

Might I do the same —
I couldn't sleep, lying on the floor
in front of a roaring fire, stirred
to toss on another log
to keep warm — the photographs
all in my head, wind and wolves
and snapping branches

nothing more

Now years later, I read about the last camera
Merton used in Bangkok the day before
he died in a freak accident when he was
electrocuted after a defective fan
fell on him

— 18 shots on a roll of 24 black
and white film, using an Alpa Reflex
a Swiss made 35 mm camera — pictures
of an edge of a building, a foreground of shore
and a body of water on a sunlit day
maybe the last glint of sun he ever saw

That camera — also a gift from Griffin —
was never used again — it landed up
at a museum, and when the curator carefully
removed it from its worn leather case
the smell of tobacco and incense filled the room

Watching the Light

It is nearly the middle of April
and not quite 8:30 at night
and I watch the last shreds
of daylight cling
to the rooftops and chimneys
and smokestacks

I believe all I need
is to reach out and capture it
keep it here for now
for a moment longer

a picture that stays
in the stillness
of dark and light

but it moves and vanishes
softly, without applause
like the sweet melody
from a radio in car
that passes by

Beauty in a Straight Line

There is beauty in that balance
drawing a straight line
letting the eye follow it from left
to right — the horizon as clean
as a new day

or so I believe as I drive south
feeling the landscape slowly relaxing —
windows down in the car
children asleep in the back

And I wonder if I might yet bump
into the clouds that have gathered
like newspapers tumbling in an open field
along that thin distant line

It's about beginnings and endings
drawing that straight line, moving
from one story to another, following
the horizon, that clean line,
seeing the balance

but why is it when I hear
my wife's dying mother whisper from
the hospital bed the beginnings and the end
are beautiful, but I say to myself
Not so much the end

Acknowledgements

The idea behind this book grew out of a conversation with John B. Lee. On a telephone call, I was telling him about how during this pandemic I was feeling a little like the great Romantic poet, William Wordsworth, because I had taken to walking and photographing in the nearby woods, and that I had come to realize that the pictures were really like the poems I was writing. They were stories. With that, John suggested that I bring the two together. I think what he revealed to me was that with one eye I was seeing pictures, and the other, I was focusing on the words to tell the same story. So, over the space of nearly a year, I wrote and dispatched these poems, and sent him photographs, one at a time, and he responded with suggestions and critiques that helped shape this manuscript into being. So, my thanks to John Lee for all the help and inspiration. I must also note the assistance of Julienne Rousseau and the keen eye of Abby Coutinho in combing through the proofs of this book.A big thanks, too, to Richard Grove for publishing this book. And to all the others in my life who have offered support and encouragement. The list is endless, but to name a few, let me include Peter Hrastovec, Ted Kloske, Howard and Jeannette Aster, Vanessa Shields, André Narbonne, Douglas MacLellan, Keith Carter, Phil Hall, Laurence Hutchman, Mary Ann Mulhern, Christopher Menard, Micheline Maylor, Susan McMaster, Rosemary Sullivan, and Karen Mulhallen.

Biographical Note

Marty Gervais is a Canadian poet, photographer, journalist, and teacher. He has won numerous awards, including the prestigious Harbourfront Festival Prize for his contributions to Canadian letters and to emerging writers, the Milton Acorn People's Poetry Prize for literature, and more than a dozen newspaper awards. His photography has appeared internationally and has been included in *American Photo* and in exhibitions, not only in Canada, but also in Ireland, France and the U.S. Marty Gervais was Windsor's first Poet Laureate and is now the city's Poet Laureate Emeritus.